TALKING TOO FAST

DAVID M BOYER

Cover design by Christopher Patchel

Author photo courtesy of Rachael Stroud

Copyright © 2018 by David M Boyer

�֎ Created with Vellum

for Rachael

ON READING SOMEONE YOU'VE NEVER HEARD OF

I took a leap. I hoped I wouldn't bruise myself too badly or break anything. But I wanted to make a start, to fold myself in metaphor and dream. No, strike that. I wanted to make little, beautiful things. That's closer. Some of them need to be picked up gently because they will try to squirm out of your hand. This is normal, but you should be ready for it. In a moment they settle down and you can examine the lacework of feathers and the fine scales. Maybe a red tongue will dart out and leave your hand with the sweet scent of something that's been living under heavy stones and only recently clawed its way to the light. But it's hard to say. I'm still in the air.

1.

The new year
a taste
of copper
in the back of my throat

a sky free of explosions

grey corridors
speed us
into
the heart
of the calendar

I'm shopping for vitamins

2.

It's picking up the pen
and seeing what happens

birds fly
branch
to lawn to branch

feathery leaves
in reverse
then fast-forward

we dream
of islands
yet to be discovered

3.

The heart is a shell on a beach

at night
you pick it up

and feel grit
in the throat for days

4.

into the great city on the train past advertisements and apartments you've seen before but couldn't recall sudden sun between buildings sudden dark underground a museum a meal a couple of people shouting down the street a far away feeling like trying to make something out across the water but not really caring what it is your feet hurt but it's still 30 more blocks should we stop at this store or another version of it in the next neighborhood the cold immense pretzels hot sugary nuts horses in winter feeling you should be walking faster though there's nowhere to go

5.

As though the rusty
parking brake

in your chest
came unstuck

you giggle
and roll downhill

colliding with
a castle
of air and soft
regret

6.

When the last
syllable
is wrung

The heat
of snow
on these hands

7.

mellow movement of her
grey muzzle this
morning of blossom when
green swirls and flexes
and writhes over yellow stubble
for the heat to come

she's restless to get out
and chase anything
and these little sentences
breathe deep into
the time when the oldest
part of the plant is the seed

8.

A dream in the unexpected
snowstorm worry about
the paper I need to write
on nanotubes
since I know nothing of the subject
other than what I have gleaned
from The Big Bang Theory

and then at the audition
unsure of whether or not
I will hit the notes
the judges
dismiss me after a single
sung syllable and I walk
slow and search for my license plate
with only the light from my phone

9.

how I walked
locked myself in this corner, but

This is a different beast
doesn't play by the rules

you once loved

The lights are too bright and
on all day

Take this razor but wait
a year and a day to follow me

10.

Always turning and always falling
making tea, remembering
dead friends and lovers, trying
not to think
like a teenager and to write
like a child

the rug curls a bit when the
humidity rises and deflates
when things dry out. Some
mornings I wake up early
and sleep all day.

11.

Someone long ago with a fine, sharp needle
and steady hand poked through this black,

making more holes than we can

count in a night, so we can look up now
and then and remember how to breathe.

12.

The cold always
with you the static

between your ears
gets louder outside
dump trucks, sound
of metal scraping metal

See how well you can roll
yourself into a ball

and hide from the dagger
that takes years to

make its way
into your soft skull

13.

The body constantly trying
to tie itself
into a knot or turn
into stone
but something stops it.

Look at any petal
& see how it's done.

14.

Birds immune
to likes and retweets

on the branch

a single song
perfected

15.

Ancient pottery asleep in the deep earth

Some shards long to be
brushed off, cleaned,
revered, iconic, important.

Others want nothing more
than the warmth of
dark places, the safety
of beginnings before beginnings.

You have to keep your hands
ready to grab it as it races past.

16.

And what if the
what ifs are always
there dancing
in dreams
lurking in cupboards
pooling under the tongue?

Will anything in these hands
ever finish with a soft click
as the key turns and we
smile to ourselves and put
the book back or will the road

ever spill out ahead
aimless and waiting, wanting
someone to sculpt its
fine eyes into
wings that will never fly

17.

Maybe the secret to the secret is not saying
that you think you found it and maybe —
but what do I know about it?
The time I've spent beneath the great
trees is small. My beard
is thin and grey and there is always
a pain in my shoulder. But in this small
coffee cup there is a future where you would
gladly pay an admission fee
just for the scent of the blossoms.

18.

I've always been afraid of suddenly teleporting
into another life thousands of miles away,

abandoned on some rock with no
way back to the warm familiar
scents and well-worn devils

where I sip my hot chocolate
and pick up another self-help book.

19.

An hour before dawn

the moon, Jupiter
and the giant Arcturus
discuss an ancient grievance.

Dogs bitten by rabid
rabbits in their dream chase

mist forming
unforming

20.

Hard to remember that the
pimple, pain, and ache don't
last for eternity. Of course, now
is eternity. But perhaps,

since it's very early, instead, I will direct
you to the advice on eating many
vegetables and drinking clean
water. If it's not me, it's you.

21.

It rained all night and into the morning.

I thought there should be a poem
in there somewhere, away from
the defeated mounds of leaf and the jewel-
heavy branches, but when I searched

the sky purple orange clouds were escaping.

22.

How quickly we get tired.
That little blue flame of our passion
gutters, then on to the next toy.

The fog covered the ground this morning
making the world look like
a scene from a monster movie.

23.

When I close my eyes I'm
floating down a long tunnel backwards.
The light takes its time returning.

On the back of an envelope
in a small script, I keep track
of when I see
a moth of any kind.

24.

Deep in the breath
there is a kind of gift
left by a mother
ancient and unknown.

As many
coins as you need
to make your wish
come true in a
fountain made of light.

25.

Some mornings there is no
poem in you. You drink coffee

eat oranges and file papers
that were once important.
You look at the bare branches

and at the pine. The animal
shapes in the clouds. Maybe

tomorrow two will
spring from this old pen.

26.

The faces appear in the carpet
as I breathe in the morning.
Sometimes lions or crocodiles,
a tired man or monstrous child.

And outside the outside
our sun toys with
us, giving and taking the light
until one day its love
won't be able to wait any more.

27.

I never wanted to be like you. I only
wanted to be me, perhaps with
a dash of Blake or Bowie.

When I wandered through
the woods I was neither
Lewis nor Clark. Still, the world
has a way of getting
under your fingernails.

So I learned to take bits
from this man and that woman
and build a kind of person.

I never fully turned right or left,
but revolving, created a kind of gravity.

28.

If I balance on the precipice
with an elbow resting on either
side, like this, will something
from the great depth reach

up and flick me with a finger,
launch me into space, or will
I get up in a few minutes with
bloody elbows longing
for a better sandwich?

29.

Much like the firefly

that delights darkened
eyes and calls back
dusty tales and future
dreams, painting the night
with little gasps of magic

sometimes it lands
on your hand and all you
can do is summon
all your strength to not
crush it in joy.

30.

If you feel you've lost your way, consider
for a moment that your way, grown
tired of your constant complaints,
doing nothing while listening to
countless TED Talks
and after long discussions
with its lawyer had decided
to leave you. This way was never
really into you and maybe you're
both better off alone.

31.

Teeth of autumn
strip the locust. The sun
comes strutting in.

Today
the softest music is
too loud,

the plainest girl
too pretty.

32.

Early morning, midweek and before
the storm the winds bend the trees.

I notice the first grey hair
above my dog's right eye.

33.

The groundhog
rests, happy as a mournful
guitar fills the world
with syrupy shadow
and aches like
chocolate cake

34.

The years drain away
and what am I still
chasing?

These loose lines
will never be fit
snares for the bright
beautiful eyes

in the dark
out of reach
of any gasping
syllable's plea

35.

Tumbling down all these
years through dark root-
filled tunnels cut by jagged
discarded words
and landing on my back

look at all those stars

36.

Not as cold as expected
and the snow, so far,
has held off on its promise
to betray the quiet fox.

.

37.

The problem deep in these
sentences. The floor
still sticky. After rain, a scent of sulphur
and the body of a crow in a field
of yellow grass.

Some say

If you come home early
I'll cook something from the old book.

38.

And the pen wants to move
to add color to the world despite
this heavy hand and black
ink the rain and this weak tea. So
much time down the drain
and never to fall from the sky again.

And if I hadn't hid here
in this bookstore I never
would have met my new love,
with her words that jump
off the page and run
madly into the fields
of new and sweet green
lately sprouted in my chest.

39.

The path is the same whether
you are submerged
in ice or have to use
a machine to speak.

Don't think I'm frosting cupcakes here.

Every day people
give up and every day people fight.

40.

by the edge of a great water I am yet to leave

how to speak
without the voices
sewn into the clothes
of memory
I try to rid myself
but the wind is cold

before this window green lawn newly
planted red and white flashes of something from
giant screens in windows across the lawn and
on the many roofs squirrels running and running

how much can I take for myself and still leave you
with enough how do I pick the right bird from
the sky to swallow this fleeting flying
fleeing thing in my chest

41.

Somewhere between a feast and a snack, but
how to know for sure
and can we teach the other animals?

I see the bright steam
that pours from the sea
through the long night
but I don't have
wings to follow it.

42.

Too much time on the easy
problems and all you have is mush.

even if you can't feel it
there is a fire deep inside

forged in an ancient sun
that never had a name.

43.

Again into darkness
as someone collects
junk to build a throne

and even if you don't see
fallen leaves as a new
door, the fact of used
books compels us

so what if I check for goblins
I've also never seen a proton

down to the river and start
the incantation again
this blood is wearing off

44.

A thousand scenarios
involving lips, guns, hips,
assorted savory goods,
stashes of cryptocurrency
not to mention the trusty
mules and guinea pigs
for the long journey
to the temple after
the ship finds safe harbor.

And a thousand more
thoughts that turn
all this to dust &
fuels our future suns.

45.

the trick
is to let
your handwriting

grow

so small

that it is
mistaken

for the internal
monologues
of ants

•

46.

Good morning. I hope
you are well. Unfortunately I tried
following all the instructions
you provided, but the device is
still not responding
or should I say not responding
correctly. Instead of accurately
recording my sleeping patterns
and weight it insists on updating me
every few minutes on the weather
in foreign cities. I will not
mention the shocks it gives me when
I try to reprogram it. Finally, it
has found a way to adopt cats
from the local shelter and seems
to think we need nearly all of them.
This may make the long
winter nights more comfortable
but does not endear me to my neighbors.
That said, I will not be returning
the unit, but rather will be moving
myself and cats to a warmer climate.
Perhaps more light on the solar
panels will correct whatever is at fault.

•

47.

Sunday morning Suicide, Sir Philip Sidney
leaves drop from a squirrel nest

some past hopes for a better day
the sunrise fails to load &

rain from leaf to leaf to blade of grass this thought
boiling inside of me no analog in nature

or future of an albatross before Coleridge
& say voices of the damned are in the wind

birds every seventh syllable sharpen the hours
the cool shadow inside skulls on a shelf

seed the clouds with a violet melody
tomorrow we'll dig a hole straight past obsolescence

48.

From deep inside the very
serious poet a line makes
me laugh out loud. Could he
was been wearing a mask all
these years? How heavy it

must grow in the days when
the light returns but the buds
are still far from
bursting on smooth branches.

49.

That moment in the deep
unbright morning
when a sound
maybe outside
maybe inside

a body as heavy
as the oldest resolutions
shifts, turns
plants a foot

50.

Picking up the blank book
I always expect fireworks or
at least a CG explosion.

Now and then a little
door opens

some slow
light creeps through
and makes a mark on this
grey flesh and for
a moment
warmth.

If the wind is blowing
in the right direction
it becomes a star.

51.

always thinking about that end
& how fast

but then
a flower from a crack in the sidewalk
nameless

your eyes from a life of looking

bees asleep, calm shape of clouds
just morning

with headaches over long
grass
swaying

I'm here to stay

the lights all red the roses hips

swallows settle for less

52.

At the end of my time
I'd like perhaps a small
monument upon which
one or two names
are engraved. But

looking now there is
a garden already
overflowing
abundantly green
upon whose many swaying
leaves are the names

of the kind ones
who shared some time, money,
attention, laughter, drinks,
before disappearing
into dark warm
corridors in the rose
heart of the story.

53.

I dump out a
half-empty cup of coffee
still warm

to show
the red
worms in my gut
who's boss

only the housefly
notices
&
raises a tiny fist

54.

If I could rush out
into this grey morning of white
snow, white sky, and collect all
the little diamond fragments

falling, I'd have
fuel for a billion poems.

55.

Susan said she didn't think I paid attention,
but when she read my stuff she wasn't sure.

Grandma said I have no oomph, just
like you're imagining it.

Karin said I should try some happier
music, ditch Joy Division for Robyn Hitchcock.

Robyn (no relation) took me
giggling up and down the
rills and trills of Gerard
M. Hopkins and the
tintinnabulation of the bells.

Eric and Ed introduced me to
Bowie on the same day, but with different tracks.

What isn't about some kind of music?

I was in a cloud of sweet smoke and laughed as

My parents said
little as they watched me
fall into a hole. I wouldn't
have listened.

I tell myself that I only
want to look forward on these
clear days, but there's a little
mouse always gnawing on the wires.

56.

and again nothing to say says the head and the fingers
forget that and run out on their own what good has this
head done lately anyway and blossoms hang on the trees so
briefly as birds sing courtship songs skyward in the
weakening dark make ready this short but wide song for an
empty page hungering for music

57.

and bad-tempered birds scold the
sprinklers sounding like an atonal symphony
that's well-respected but no one listens to
and yes the light seems to be going
from my eyes as the
full stop from the language
or maybe the clouds are
trying to message me or send
some clear candy and sure you
think it's all worthwhile
but when did you return to the
musty halls with your
action figure in hand as
large as a giant's nightmare
to rule the world with a piece
of toast smeared with cheap jam

I lie on the floor and wonder if it's yesterday yet

58.

my boss a collector of insomniacs walks the halls on stilts
examines every coffee cup for signs of progress and avoids
the stairs today is Friday so we will have our nails cut when
we hear the yelping we instinctively check the progress of
our 401(k)s and count the leaves of the cypress our greatest
asset in a moment the weekend will begin and the dreams
we share shift to images of pirate ships chained to a
monstrous wave of silver fish

59.

with thousands of me gripping earth
warm tasty wet with rock and worker
worm making space
above the light hurts but I
reach and reach for it
in every way
it fills me with such goodness
I split and swell
in little ways &
gift the soil
that bit of me
that starts again

60.

The trick is flying into
your body the right way

Too fast and the world
blurs, colors merge
and you grit your teeth
to powder

Too slow and the you
you aim for is long gone
by the time you get there

Watch the birds on the lawn
and before long you'll
know how to keep the
secret

61.

the dog's sideways glance
from a little plush bed

                                        let's go kill a small
                                        animal—what fun!

but my hands are cold &

old words fall from my
moss-filled mouth

62.

you, marble-colored
horse in the steady rain
standing your ground
carefully chewing as I
speed by in a green car

aching for home

63.

the town changes but begrudgingly
an angry hand-painted sign on the side
of a house in black and white

old ransacked green hills look
over abandoned churches factories small
homes packed tight on narrow streets
as though the land were precious to you

shingles peeling off mustard colored and
wait someone lives here after all

swallows purple martins catbirds blue jays
robins the unshakeable sparrow tapestry
of song new made dawnly sunsetly

bric-a-brac shops lawn ornaments homemade
jam sitting rooms rusted cars bric-a-brac

behind a fence dogs who bark when you're
miles away and stand still watching
waiting then back to the little house

crumbling rough stone walls covered in
moss same as when I was seven

64.

in that other future where you were not there to help and she fell and gone and you walked the years alone and never saw those facebook posts of her cakes and concert nights the short hot silences and the smile that came around so quick you didn't deserve it.

65.

Another day and dawn
so what will
we do with this clay
it can be shaped
into bowls or stones
or left where it's warm

in the no-income housing
for cousins who never
developed bones
I'll finish my coffee
and have a shower

66.

the water still too hot and no apology forthcoming I take
some shady words down the smooth burrow and examine
the tiny shelves I find there with centuries-old mugs and
polished bone tools and once I have soaked up the musty
air I return to my contemporaries ready for any insult

67.

the cold
so cold it feels like
fire then
in the first moment

of spring
all is forgiven
as the mind

of a butterfly
springs from
the sharp margin
of retreating snow

68.

They say
there's something in
someone's nothing and nothing
in someone's something or something

and last night in a dream I visited a dream shop
that I had been to on a night
many nights ago with some other friend
after a long voyage by boat a tedious voyage by car
moments of panic with the GPS & into
the ancient beauty of this dream Philadelphia
with massive crumbling stone Buddhas
free river transport unending food trucks

In the shop this friend from high school opens a case
of delicately carved jade masks
pipes tablets and grabs a square to examine
before tossing it back
I tell him jade will change color in contact with skin and
even in dreams I'm a know-it-all and he points out the
pieces he thinks are terrible
I tell him about all the books
I had to give away to move here

69.

black fish through
narrow channels over
rock and root with
needle teeth gleaming
in the small hours of the mind

I ignore the threat of wolves and
I feel like I can't go on but

70.

Here comes that line
of flurries the weatherman
mentioned and despite
our history with him
we listen and prepare

and you could end the poem
there, but this bright and bracing
morning and there
are any number of hot beverages
I could enjoy before getting
in the car and flipping on NPR
on this happy Friday of the spirit.

71.

those few
warm words
from her

and I can go weeks without breakfast

72.

Now that the sun burns my skin
so quickly and the light takes all
my strength, the sunrise becomes
precious. Each shade of pink
and blue becomes a feast.

I no longer want to deceive
you with this, but to speak
clearly with a voice like light
scattered by a diamond.

73.

There's a hint of mint in the cup
from yesterday's tea. I think of my teachers
who have died. The ones I argued with and
loved and thought I knew more than and
ignored for far too long and too late now.

The wind slaps rain into tall trees
and they dance. Inside, all my
plants are on life-support.

74.

The moment in the black sky
when the color just starts
to bleed into the million

million shades of everyday
as a dream escapes

still warm
from your hungry head
into the wood

75.

I can smell grandma's
instant coffee
somewhere in this summer
afternoon she would fill their
cups right to the rim
and grandpa not
picking his up but bending

his mustache down for the first
slurp and the cancers she
beat three times and I never
got that blue radio that she
said had my name on a
sticker on the bottom

& now pyramids
of horse chestnut blossoms
thread a scent like honey
past fences falling down

76.

Organizing what's left for whoever comes next I feel a small
fear grow for this reflection but he knew what he signed up
for still the amount of wasting re: words must be addressed
at a future meeting but not the next one we'll call your
number out when the firing squad has time for you we
know you're in a rush and we appreciate your patience
could be a sentence used to teach kids the difference
between you're and your but mostly it goes over their heads
and the instinct is to treat it all every syllable as precious
and why not sure the noise of words has been shown to
never fully disintegrate and at the same time I can no longer
hear Geoffrey Chaucer entertaining his guests still you have
to be still and say your thanks for whatever words come
your way even in the city this is after all the fuel that our
pens run on though not literally of course that would be
absurd and yes I meant most of that and who let you in
anyway

77.

Winding slow through mountain woods
the clouds push stone
that crumbles for centuries.

Our tour guide's tenses get lost.

Persephone is going underground
and eating the seeds, Xerxes
lands again on the mainland and clever
Odysseus has a plan
to see his wife in a bit.

78.

The ambient soundtrack of my failures sometimes seems a
too-generous gift from some creature with bright wings and
a thousand thousand eyes.

that word you abandoned fossilized in fading letters
the word you're afraid of floating in the lake

the rush of air conditioning a bus passes hot breath
the sigh of a sponge long dry as water hits it

79.

We have all had that dream —
a dead dog slides down an
incline to the sea
and an oddly familiar
stranger in a hat appears
and drinks your tea —

Part of me thinks that we'll
never get to the message
behind the message.

Insects have made
a home in your long bones.

80.

The rain ends but the ground
refuses to green. We want to go
back to sleep. Somewhere out there
a flower is hatching a plan, a goose
is getting fed up with scraps of
yellow grass and tadpoles probe
cloudy water. The pen scratches
furious to keep up.

81.

Reading Rimbaud in middle age
a dream of high school. The colors
brighter, actions precise. The sun through
the hair of a girl I may have loved
writes a verse in the snow and the town
cries years before the shops close and those
friends who are now lost join together for
one more video game and for a moment
we believe the lie.

82.

Sure, you can start anywhere but when the credits roll, and with your taste for unwholesome pleasures—now I forgot what I was going to say. Consider the daisies. No, not that. Just wait a minute. This pain in my chest will pass, but the cramped handwriting...

They say those new condominiums are built on plans based on the movement of as yet unexplored clusters of stars where the one you loved relocated to work on that dance she was always talking about over hot milky coffee in the days when smoking was ok

83.

the office one step closer to finishing its work
and goes to sleep to dream of the Broadway
lights and a little show based on its life
where the screams and sighs are
replaced by catchy rhymes and people
pay to come inside.

84.

by midweek my senses
sludge at the bottom
of the coffee pot

(to pry my eyes open I need more
almonds and a paste made from the last
animal to pass by her open
window when the stars midwintered)

of course the faith
these days is all in
likes, retweets
and crypto stuff, but

if we can keep a few lines under
our protection
the future may yet forgive

85.

All those great ideas that
evaporate into the faint electric
interstates and gravel paths
of the mind. The dog
chews a toy and looks out the window

asking for nothing. There must
be something more. But then, why
trust the brain's propaganda? You know
what it does when you sleep.

86.

That day when you wake & it's all over—
every dream smashed, hope spilled
all over the floorboards, every breath labored.

What a glorious day!

As you open the window and step
out on the ledge & hear the cars
and wind whipping your ears, how
lucky to have such a future before you.

87.

There's a song somewhere in there
but I grip the pen too tight.

In the morning after the storm
an empty nest on wet ground.

88.

As we were taking apart the machine
that killed him, to be sent over the sea
to a place of fire and liquid metal,
I held a cog, unable to tell if
its perfume was blood or rust.

89.

late spring
a leaf

luxuriously

lets itself fall
before it has to

the new glasses have finally arrived

90.

What to make of the black branches broken and
if I say why no they're inside
what to do with that and it's true I don't have any
elaborate declarations or magnificent
coordinates into which I can recede and
study old texts with black birds
rising from the thin necks of glass flasks
and yes I'm always about to lose the
thread but I have no one to blame
and maybe tomorrow will be fine
today the sky is Turkish coffee
without sugar and those broken
branches crawl out of my throat
and don't know where to go from there

91.

When you lose your/ wallet/ you go a bit/ mad. First/ you check pants jackets laundry/ recycling bins/ aching for a glimpse./ The twisting in the stomach. You/ brush up on/ the stages of grief./ You look under pillows, shoes, in half-forgotten boxes/ in the attic/ your wife's purse your colleague's/ coffee cup. An unshakeable sense/ that it's just around some/ untroubled corner. Is/ this confirmation/ of our lot or some/ irritating lesson?/ A week later I know/ I have to put my search aside, though/ I remember hearing that/ around the edges/ of black holes, where/ all manner/ of matter is/ irretrievably collected crushed/ and turned into an infinitely/ fine paste, that particles/ and antiparticles/ now and then jump/ out in perfect pairs/ and collide, exploding/ instantly, minutely/ though sometimes/ who knows how/ one escapes/ fate and sails/ off into the real

92.

I force it like sharp
liquid from a small green fruit

these lichen memories
never make it
to my manifesto

the name you call it
making up a second a third

days of flowers
gone
but those
painted toes
I praise

blindly through winter
thin fingers of tall trees

like seeds in a fig she says no

93.

but moves before you get the shot
& the dog insists
she knows the way

the feeling that
with a bit more
the gates will part

strange verbs in an
otherwise empty head

sun on white marble, yellow flowers
by the steps, thrum of waves

the temple of Zeus in ruins

94.

Still, that scent in mid-spring
almost honey on sauntering wind

and yet my scrawl refuses to be
anything but small

95.

The bits of wet coffee grain
and strips of orange peel
that fall out of my body

to be collected and molded
into the last
sunset we will ever enjoy

96.

words to make you sound smarter:

somniloquent
anachthonistic
bathyphilic
no

97.

Polyphemus whose
name means rich with
song and story
blinded by nobody then
this name hung
on a jawless crab
not a crab
whose tail is a sword

and why do you ask
each leaf keeps us company
each cry is answered
eventfully
as the tide

98.

Some days in the bright sun
as you run in the light breeze

the horde close behind

mangled fingernails
lidless eyes, groans
and the sticky sound of muscle
and entrails exposed
to the air and dragged along

it occurs to you
Robert Frost was right
about so many things

99.

6:30 am honeyed light lingers on the tips of locust trees I
write you a thousand lines and you're gone before

(chicory on the margins
and herons, dots of fishermen
at high tide & how little tufts of cloud
a sponge and pink ink at evening...)

I describe you again and again adding subtracting praise
flower garlands translucent gems with fiery hearts and in
the end cross it all out except your name

that elementary particle of us
far from — and always will be — perfect

100.

all my life I've been writing and hoping
one day words will fall
like puzzle pieces into place

but I wonder if it's like
car keys the moment
you stop looking
you hear that jingle and
they're in your pocket

a poem should have flowers perhaps nothing else

but like this slice of bread with cashew butter,
you devour and forget about it

and that means you've arrived and can start work

but clean off those dirty hands
there's something else I want to show you

www.ingramcontent.com/pod-product-compliance
Lightning Source LLC
Chambersburg PA
CBHW070641030426
42337CB00020B/4118